Acknowledgments

Les Davies M.B.E, F.R.G.S
For input and guidance through the process.

TREE TALK

Dedicated

My Dear Les Davies. Our love of trees,
enjoyable walks in Glastonbury Abbey
inspired the writing of this book.

TREE TALK
Contents

TREE TALK

Mother Earth take my seed
Bury me deep, so I may breed
Sapling roots thrive in the ground
Grow a trunk that's Heaven bound
Send me rain so I may flourish
Feed my center so I can nourish
Grow branches long with many leaves
Rustling sounds from a gentle breeze
That shakes the tree for leaves to fall
Other trees they hear the call
I need their strength to stand up high
As I reach up tall towards the sky
Autumn time there's many colours
Fall to the ground like rainbow lovers
Raindrops fall some change to snow
Now it's time to go back down below

Introduction

Since the beginning of time myths and legends have woven fables of people talking with the trees. Stories passed down throughout generations are generally based on some form of reality. So could it be there is some truth in these stories? Do trees talk? We connect with an Earthly world every day that feeds our life force. When we come into contact with Nature we have a physical energy exchange through chemical reactions which imprints on our subconscious. A walk in Nature feeds our soul leaving us exhilarated, energised and rejuvenated. So, what happens between the tree and the human to create such feelings of wellbeing? Is there a form of conversation going on between the two? In this book we will explore the way humans interact with trees. What happens within the energy exchange between trees and people? Is there a type of conversation occurring? We will explore if and how this could be possible.

We know that trees support each other and converse through chemical reactions. Is it possible that trees can support humans in a similar manner? In the same way as we talk to each other sharing ideas, thoughts and words. We chat to a friend to ease our problems; to enrich our physical, mental and emotional wellbeing - to feel happy and healthy. In the same way a walk in Nature can improve our wellbeing. So, are we subconsciously talking and interacting with trees in a similar way as we do with humans? Is it so far removed from the stories of myth and fable? That's a crazy idea I hear you mutter?! How does that work, prove it?!

History of the tree and mankind

Once upon a time humans lived in balance and harmony within the Natural world. The 'Hunter Gatherer' would take only what they needed to survive. Aboriginal Tribes that live in central Australia and the Indigenous Tribes in the Amazon still live in this way. The Ecosystem of the world changed dramatically when the Hunter Gatherer decided to settle on the land and become 'Farmers'. Settlements meant people no longer had to risk life when hunting. Animals were now held captive and reproduced to feed the human. Instead of hunting, time was now given to working the land and producing crops. Trees were cleared, and the land was tilled, to produce vegetables and feed livestock. This is called 'plagioclimax', when humans control the landscape instead of Nature. Yet trees have adapted and developed throughout the ages to continue to exist and remain dominant within the ecosystem. Many landscapes within our natural environment would still be covered with trees, if it remained untouched by mankind. Trees work together to maintain a dominant role within Nature to survive, whilst supporting the surrounding community that they live in, feeding their precious nutrients to shrubs, plants and fungi. Even when they die they create a space in the woodland canopy for more saplings to grow, providing fresh ground for all shrubs and plant life to renew and thrive. The strongest and most hardy, will survive and claim territory. This is called climatic succession, as the change within the plant growth affects the natural succession of the ecosystems. Hence the saying if one tree fell down in the Amazon jungle it would have a great effect on its surrounding ecosystem. Trees are generally long lived and will grow strong for hundreds, sometimes thousands of years. Humans are but a pinprick on their timeline.

Trees living as a community

Woodlands hold a sense of community. Yes, trees have the capacity to support, protect and communicate with each other as well as the surrounding plant life. Some call it the 'wood-wide web' that connects the trees underground through fungal networks. This is how trees share water, nutrients and communicate information. For example, if a tree is withering, other trees will support it by sending sap that is stored in the trunk, down the root system and through fine, hairlike root tips that join to the microscopic fungal filaments which link up with the roots of the nearby tree. At the same time this transition provides the fungi with the sugar it requires to grow, so an exchange is made in the process. This is how the trees feed young saplings which are unable to access daylight and would die without sap to create chlorophyll. Old trees that have fallen are often fed in this way too - this support helps them to survive. Trees will also support each other during external invasions, such as disease or insect attacks. A tree will excrete gas that repels insects. This is done by producing jasmonic acid, a plant hormone Ethylene (C_2H_4), a gas that moves between the cells of the tree. During a drought, Ethylene gas will evaporate into the air to prevent other plants from growing. This enables the tree to claim its territory and maintain the supply of water in order to survive. Scientists have recently found that trees send slow pulsing electrical signals through the root system, which is similar to a nervous system of a human. By these means trees are communicating with each other all the time. So, is there a way for a tree to communicate with animals and humans in a similar way? Scientists have found that animals can smell when a tree is unwell. Is it possible that a tree can sense a human is unwell and needs support? Let's explore the possibilities by first understanding the life of a tree.

Science root system of a tree

Humans have evolved over thousands of years and we consider ourselves an intelligent, supreme life form, above the animal kingdom and plant life. Yet, we still rely on both of them for our food. A tree only needs earth, water and sunlight to survive. A seed falls onto the ground from the tree. Through favourable conditions it becomes embedded into the ground. Shoots then form as the seed is fed with nutrients from the surrounding soil. Now as a sapling it burrows further into the ground. Next a root system is created that grows and develops into a trunk. Water carries nutrients up from the ground which are transported through the trunk system. As the tree continues to grow stronger, the survival intelligence of the tree splits into pathways producing many branches. As the light frequencies shine down from the sun and combine with the nutrients at the tip of the branch, many leaves sprout. Chloroplasts absorb light from the sun rays which then combine with water and carbon dioxide gas forming a vital chemical 'Chlorophyll'. This process is called 'photosynthesis'. This forms carbohydrates that are then stored in the trunk system as starch. Sucrose is then formed which combines with water and nutrients creating 'sap'. The tree will hold onto its leaves in Autumn for as long as possible in order to produce sucrose, as this enables it to store large amounts of sap in the root system which will feed the tree during the winter. The change in season will bring rougher weather that will strip the branches of leaves. Bacteria and fungi then feed on the decomposed leaves and the process of transporting the nutrients starts all over again. When the tree eventually dies it completely decomposes back into the earth providing nutrients for surrounding plant life. So do the trees feed humans with nutrients and positive ions when we walk in the woodland?

Root system of a human

The human body is extremely complex. Many systems interact together; circulatory, digestive, respiratory, endocrine, reproductive, nervous, muscular and urinary. But what exactly is the fundamental source that ensures the body to continue to work? Nutrients like sodium, calcium, potassium and magnesium have a specific electrical charge called ions. Our cells conduct electrical currents through the body. So, does this work as a kind of internal network, similar to that which a tree benefits from, and which interconnects with the Natural World? Traditional Chinese Medicine (TCM) may be able to give some insight to this question. TCM has evolved over many thousands of years. The Chinese observed how people's day to day life and the interactions with the external world will determine how the body functions internally on a physical, mental or emotional level. Anything that is dysfunctional in an individual's life will create an imbalance in the energy system of the body. TCM philosophy is based around an energy circuit which moves in lines throughout the body connecting to the internal organs. These are called meridian lines of which there are 12 in total. Energy is not static; it moves and flows, and in order to do so needs two poles, as in the positive and negative connections in electricity, so it may move from one point to the other. The Chinese called this polarity yin and yang. Everything follows this pattern in life and is constantly in a state of ebb and flow. So, is this energetic network of the human meridian system able to connect with the electrical pulses given off by trees through their 'wood-wide web? Allowing the trees to sense when we need support. Considering this question from an Eastern philosophies perspective, may give us some more answers?! Eastern philosophy believes that all life force is connected and they use the 5 Elements of Nature to demonstrate how this is possible.

5 Elements of Nature

Thousands of years ago the practice of Traditional Chinese Medicine arose, as it was observed that the 5 Elements of the surrounding ecosystem had an effect on the health of a patient. The 5 Elements encompass all the necessary requirements for humanity to survive on this planet. Air (oxygen), Wood (Spirit or essence), Water (moisture), Earth (soil) and Fire (heat). TCM practitioners use the 5 Elements to diagnose any imbalance in a patient. Trees interconnect all of the 5 Elements hence why it is often referred to as the Tree of Life. Fire is represented by the sun rays that create energy via photosynthesis for a tree and Vitamin D in a human. Earth is required for the seeds of vegetables to grow and to provide a foundation for the root of the tree to grow and feed. Water is the substance that makes up the largest part of the tree through the centre of the trunk, similarly just as humans are made of two-thirds of water. Wood is considered as the

Spirit of the tree, the trunk is the core stability. Humans originally relied on wood for warmth and making a home and is now used for many resources. Air represents the breathing system in a human and trees, the exchange system that transforms air to oxygen. Trees and humans are interconnected through the 5 elements.

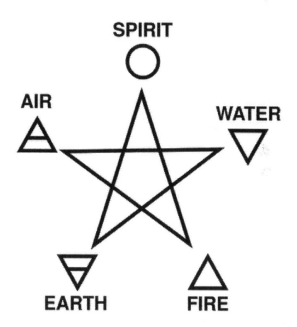

Chakra system in a human

Eastern philosophy looks at the human body in a completely different way from the Western world. Indian vedics believe the body functions from 7 energy centres in the body called the chakra system. The invisible chakras cannot be seen by the human eye but can be sensed and felt as the energy is emitted from the body. The meridian lines are connected to these energy centers. Each physical system in the body has a paired meridian. Yin and yang, positive and negative ions. Like the electrical box in a house that charges electricity through cables to a plug socket. The chakras charge electrical energy through the meridians to the various pressure points around the body. The pressure points are where a trained Acupuncturist would place needles to stimulate any stuck energy throughout the meridian. Acupressure works in a similar way. Imagine if you needed to clear a blocked hose pipe. If you placed pressure on either side of the blockage the pressure of air flow would unblock the stuck area and water would flow again. This is how acupressure can help to create health and wellbeing. When the energy is blocked dis-ease and ailments occur. This is why acupuncture and acupressure are effective treatments to ease painful symptoms. When the energy of the meridians and chakras are balanced the body is grounded and healthy. The chakras project the energy from the body and we sense and feel the energy of others.

Meridians and ley lines

Many Eastern philosophies believe that all living beings are interconnected and are all part of the same energy structure. It is believed that the world is connected by this invisible source, the 'chi' that flows through all life on Earth. Can one energetic source connect everything? Scientists now agree that the same core DNA structure is in all living organisms on Earth, and yes, this includes humans.

The Earth itself is considered to have energy portals, chakras and meridians called 'ley lines'. This would suggest that life is interconnected in every way. So, are the ley lines of the Earth similar to the meridian system that the Chinese have identified within humans? Do the electrical pulses within the roots of trees connect with both the human meridian system and the ley lines of the Earth? Could this be the way trees communicate with humans? And can we sense this energetic process?

The auric energy field

Science has proven that the body gives off an energy transmission, a glowing energy field known as an aura. There are many ways we can experience feeling this invisible energy. For example if you walk into a room, we can feel from a distance if a person is warm or cold in personality. Without even talking to a person we can feel what mood or frame of mind they are in, be it angry, sad or happy. Are we sensing each other through the electrical pulses transmitting out from the chakras? Do we send out an energy vibration into the world? Can we see the auric field? Qi Gong is a Chinese exercise that works with the auric field by moving the body very slowly into a series of positions or postures. One of the starting exercises is to sense what Chinese call 'qi', by collecting this energy field between the hands. You can try it for yourself. Firstly, rub the hands together and hold the hands a short distance apart in front of the navel of the body.

Slowly move the palm of the hands to meet. Then slowly move the hands about a foot apart again. Repeat this three or four times. Each time you will feel an electrical energy building up, 'qi' energy. Eventually you will feel you have a resistance and that there is a ball of energy between the hands. We can also see this energy. On a summer's day if we relax our gaze onto the horizon we will see the 'heatwaves'. Using the same method we can do a similar exercise to see the auric field of the tree. So, if we can see and feel this energy can we hear it too?

Sound vibration

Scientists have now proven that all plants vibrate a sound at a very high frequency. Something we cannot hear but that we can sense. It is known that Traditional Aboriginal Tribes lived off the land in the bush for long periods of time from what would appear barren land. To source food and water they would simply lie on the Earth with their ear to the ground. This way they could feel the vibration of animals walking on the Earth or hear water moving underground. They are known to communicate with members of the Tribe that go out hunting, purely from connecting with high pitched sounds. Indigenous Tribes will often chant and dance, and to our Western world that all looks a bit strange! But why do they do this? Elders from the Tribe will tell you they are connecting with the vibration of Nature. Sending out sound via the vocal cords when chanting and sending a vibration into the ground whilst dancing. When people meditate you will often hear them chant the 'OM' mantra. This may appear strange for anyone unaccustomed to meditation techniques. So, why do they make this sound and what has this to do with trees? The meditater will focus on releasing the 'OM' sound to connect and clear a vibration from each chakra. The individual's vibration is released via the vocal cords and out into the ecosystem. Each chant will resonate a different frequency connecting with the diverse vibrations in Nature. The aim of meditation is to connect the inner energy of the individual to the outer world. Sound is an expression of our own personal inner world. We express our emotions, energetically giving our words meaning by the varied sound vibrations as we speak. We project our thoughts and feelings, from our inner world through the energy vibration of sound. We have lost the ability to understand that every thought, word, movement and action, we are giving out a vibration that is connected with Nature.

Connect the 5 senses with trees

Forest air feels fresher than city air but it isn't simply because there are no car fumes. Scientific evidence shows that time spent in a green space reduces stress levels and blood pressure within 3 minutes. So what is happening to cause this change in people? As we walk amongst the trees we breathe out carbon dioxide into the air that the tree transforms into oxygen. As we breathe in the oxygen provided by the trees we take in the smell, the essence of the tree. Trees release Natural essential oils to protect themselves from germs and insects. These are called phytoncides. As we inhale the Natural oils in the air, the body relaxes and the immune system is boosted. Besides this therapeutic effect on the body, walking through woodland stimulates the five senses of touch, sight, hearing, smell and taste. The colours of trees, woodlands, countryside or a garden are soothing to the eyes. As a breeze moves through the trees the rustling of the leaves has a soothing effect on the hearing. There is often fruit to taste from trees and plants. Nowadays many people enjoy touching a tree. We interact through our senses. What we smell, see, hear and touch creates a chemical reaction within ourselves and the surrounding environment. A form of communication is occurring with every interaction through chemical exchange. So are we subconsciously talking and interacting with trees? Let's explore further by using scientific techniques and learn to interact with the tree community. You can try it yourself!

'Forest bathing'

The Japanese practise of 'forest bathing' sitting or standing under a tree, is scientifically proven to improve health in humans. A public health programme in Japan called this act 'shinrin-yoku' and is now promoted as a therapy. Shinrin means 'forest' and yoku means 'bath'. The concept is to bathe in the atmosphere of the forest absorbing Nature through the senses. Try 'forest bathing' for yourself and connect with the trees. Find a quiet space and choose a tree. Sit with your back in line with the trunk of the tree connecting with the bark. Keep your bare feet flat on the ground and close your eyes. You will feel the negative ions in your energy field falling away as your energy grounds. The tree will feed energy up through your feet. You can visualise stress and negative thoughts falling through the ground. Sit and allow the energy exchange till you feel the 'switch'. From feeling separate from the tree and the Earth, you will feel connected. Listen to the rustling in the trees as the breeze shakes the leaves together, smell the fragrance that the tree emits and breath in the fresh air to fill your lungs with oxygen. Feel the bark of the tree and the texture of the leaves. The eyes relax and take in the beautiful colours. The body responds by increased parasympathetic nervous system activity which invokes rest, conserves energy and slows down the heart rate, lowering blood pressure, reducing the stress hormone production that boosts the immune system and improves overall feelings of wellbeing.

Tree Talk Meditation

Another way to connect with the tree is to meditate. Do not let the word meditation discourage you. To meditate, is to simply sit or stand quietly and still. The tree you choose is important as it will have the Essence of energy that you require, to feed your being at that moment in time. Stand by the first tree you are drawn too. At first you will feel separate from the tree. Once relaxed, you will start to feel mesmerised by the tree. At some point the 'switch' moment will occur. This is when you have the feeling of being connected to Nature. The more you gaze upon the tree you will feel changes within your body. You feel relaxed, your head is clearer, you feel rejuvenated and energised. You may feel emotions releasing. New ideas may come into your mind. The tree will interact with you by sending positive ions into the atmosphere. Continue to absorb the Essence of the tree connection. Another form of 'switch' will occur. This time you will feel it on a more physical level as the tree sends energy underground to connect with the human root system. If it feels an imbalance in a neighbouring tree it will send the required nutrients and positive ions, in order to continue the growth and health of the surrounding ecosystem. The tree will interact with you as it would with other trees in its vicinity. Your legs may feel shaky as the energy works its way up through the meridian system in the body. After a few minutes you will feel grounded, energetically anchored to the Earth. This is when we are truly connected with Nature.

Tree Medicines

Since time began trees have been recognised for their healing powers. Egyptians, Aboriginals, Pagans have worshipped 'The Tree of Life' for its medicinal properties for thousands of years. Places like the Amazon Rainforests still have Indigenous Tribes that are connected with the Earth's energy. Indigenous Tribal Elders called shaman have the knowledge to heal by using herbs, plants and tree bark from the Essence of the tree. Shamans have the ability to connect with the vibrational sound from plant life. Their fine tuned senses allow them to connect with the high frequencies of plants, herbs and trees. They listen to their intuition and the vibrational sound of the Earth to show them which plants will heal an ailment. Pharmaceutical companies have connected with shamans from Indigenous Tribes in order to learn which plants they use in their healing practice. Scientists have then broken down the chemical compounds in plants to learn to use the natural healing properties in trees to produce many household medications for common ailments. The most popular is willow bark that contains a substance commonly known as Aspirin used for pain relief in humans. Further science created more powerful treatments for people with more serious ailments. Such as chemicals from the pine tree bark that produces Pycnogenol, which helps against deep vein thrombosis. Cinchona tree bark contains quinine which is used in anti malarial drugs. Yew trees are the source of Taxol that is used in cancer treatment. Holistic companies aim to use the Natural Essence of the trees, for example, tea tree oil is useful for skin infections. Pollen from a tree is used in pollen tablets to counteract Hayfever. Holistic tree Essence is given orally as a tincture on the tongue for mental and emotional health. So what health issues can tree Essence help with in humans?

Essence of the oak tree

The Oak tree Essence is for people who work too hard, who never give in or admit their limitations. Even when exhausted they are driven to carry on regardless. The Oak tree will connect with your energy to rejuvenate and relax you. If you 'forest bath' under this tree you will feel energised yet relaxed. Oak trees generally live for many years and have deep roots so have a very solid, grounding effect on the body.

Essence of a willow tree

The willow tree Essence is for people who have become resentful, inflexible and bitter or exhibit the tendency to blame others. Often this type of person will see themselves as a victim. The willow tree is all about flexibility and flow, think of a willow tree next to a pond bending over the water without breaking. Fences are made from the willow due to its flexibility. Willow bark is used in pain relief; Aspirin releases stiffness in the body creating more flexibility. 'Tree bathing' under a willow tree near flowing water will always help to unwind, relax and enable you to see the world in a less stressed way. Willow Essence will help you to forgive, let go of anger and take responsibility for our actions in life.

Essence of a beech tree

People who need the help of Beech Essence are generally very strong individuals who find it difficult to cope with how other people behave. They become irritable and short fused. The Essence of the beech tree will help them to be more understanding and tolerant towards others and to accept them for all that they are, even when their behaviour is intolerant. The beech tree will draw you to it for some 'tree bathing' when you are experiencing tricky situations in life.

Seasons of Nature

People who live close to the Earth understand the importance of Nature. Each year as Nature works through the process of adapting to each change in season, so does a human. All of Nature works hand in hand with the seasonal transitions of the cycle of life and responds internally and externally on every level in a similar way.

Spring : After shedding all of its leaves and closing down for the winter the tree begins the renewal process. All the water, sugars and nutrients it has stored within its root system over winter are now pumped back up the tree to grow leaves and start the photosynthesis process. For humans Spring is a time of renewal. The sun rays bring people outdoors and the body feels more active and energised.

Summer: With the maximum daylight hours the tree harvests every bit of sunlight that it can to send food back into the root system and draws up massive amounts of water. Summer is the time of fertility as the tree grows its fruit. The tree now in full bloom will create a canopy to protect many surrounding plants from the harsh sun rays. On a sunny day people sit under a tree to prevent overheating. Humans make the most of the sun to boost the immune system with vitamin D from the sunrays, to prevent catching viruses in the winter months.

Autumn: Daylight hours begin to shorten and the tree hangs onto its leaves as long as possible. Conifers who live in colder climates and retain leaf cover all year round, can pump their own version of antifreeze into the leaves. Autumn is when any fruits that the tree has produced are dropped to the ground maintaining its strength for the winter. Humans feed off the fruit upping the Vitamin C levels that create a stronger immunity for the winter months.

Winter: Time now to close down and conserve energy for the regrowth in the Spring. This applies to trees and humans.

A Tree

I think that I shall never see
Anything as lovely as a tree
A tree that looks at God all day
And lifts its leafy arms to pray
A tree who may in summer wear
A nest of birds within its hair
A tree that gives us air to breath
And shakes its leaves in summer breeze
A tree that shines with Autumn glow
The leaves that fall before the snow
A tree that sprays the air with scent
To heal our wounds is Heaven sent
The tree of life we honour its grace
As it's presence feeds the human race

Epilogue

So, returning to the question at the beginning of the book, do Trees Talk with humans? Scientists are gradually managing to provide tangible evidence of what our Ancient world has known for many years. It appears we are all interconnected. Fed by one energy source. So you see we are very much like trees. Mankind lives hand in hand with Nature. I guess the answer is we may not talk the same language, but we definitely connect and support each other on many levels. The aim of this book is to pass on knowledge and help you learn to use your intuition and senses to connect with Nature at a deeper level. Then you can decide for yourself if we talk with trees. I hope you have enjoyed the book and that it enhances your health as you connect with the tree essence. And, for a bit of fun I have included how to figure out a tree's age and height.

Enjoy

How to estimate the age of a tree

Estimating the age of a tree can be done by counting the annual growth rings across the tree trunk. All well and good if the tree has been felled, but how can you estimate the age of a standing tree? Here is a simple method. Measure the circumference of the chosen tree at chest height. This can be done with a tape measure, or much more fun is to use the distance between your outstretched arms. This should be about the same as your height but not always. Get someone to measure you up! So, stretch out your arms around the tree and continue till you arrive back at the first point. Example if you are 6ft tall and you stretch out your arms twice that is 12ft. Multiply 12 x 12 = 144 years old.

1" = 1 year growth, 25mm = 1 year growth

44

Measuring the height of a tree

For this you need an assistant! Take a stick, or even a pencil and move backwards holding it upright until the height of the tree matches your chosen measure. Then turn your stick or pencil on its side parallel with the ground and get your assistant to walk away from the tree until they reach the end of your measure. The distance between them and the tree is its height. If they then walk towards the tree counting the distance in feet whilst walking to the trunk base. This is the measure of the tree.

Much more fun is to keep bending down and looking through your legs for the top of the tree. When you can just see it, you have completed a right angle triangle. This gives you an approximate 45 degree sighting of the top. The distance between you and the tree is its height!

References:

Tree Poem is adapted from Joyce Kilmer's poem by Les Davies, MBE, FRGS and Julie M. Somerville

The Miracle of Trees by Olavi Huikari, (2012)

Shinrin-Yoku, The Art and Science of Forest Bathing by Dr Qing Li, (2018)

Kitchen Pharmacy by Rose Elliot Carlo de Paoli, (1991)

The Hidden Life of TREES by Peter Wohlleben, (2015)

2nd Edition, Traditional Acupuncture, The Law of the Five Elements by Dianne M. Connelly, P.H.D, (1994)

YouTube: Down to Earth (documentary) (shamans)

For further information on
Julie M. Somerville,
BA (hons) Health Studies,
B.S.Shiatsu Practitioner,
B.S.Y Nutrition

Glastonbury books/walks/tours
Email: info@glastoexperience.co.uk
Website: www.glastoexperience.co.uk

Printed in Great Britain
by Amazon